In the
FLOWER GARDEN
with
PERCY THROWER

After four years at the Royal Gardens, Windsor, Percy Thrower started his career in public parks. In 1946 he moved to Shrewsbury, where ever since he has been Parks Superintendent.

For the past eight years Mr Thrower has conducted a regular series of gardening programmes on the BBC Midland Regional programme, and during the past four years has made Gardening Club on Television a most popular feature, for he and his guests show viewers exactly how to do the many seasonal tasks in the garden.

In the
FLOWER GARDEN
with
PERCY THROWER

OF TELEVISION GARDENING CLUB

LONDON

W. H. & L. COLLINGRIDGE LIMITED

*First published in 1957
by W. H. & L. Collingridge Ltd.
Tavistock Street, London, W.C.2
Printed and bound in Great Britain
by Hazell Watson & Viney Ltd.
Aylesbury and London*

CONTENTS

ILLUSTRATIONS

JANUARY

MOST gardeners, like so many other people, make their New Year resolutions, you know. I suppose the most common one will be to try to grow better fruit, flowers and vegetables than last year. That is usually the aim of anyone who is keen on their garden, we are always trying to do something better—that is half the fun of it. If this is one of your New Year resolutions, then preparations for the coming seasons must begin right away. During any very open weather most of the winter digging should have been completed. A job for the dark winter evenings is to make out a list of your seed requirements for the year; this is a fireside job. Order early and you will be sure of getting the kinds and varieties you want. Order only the best and from a reliable seedsman; there is more to be lost than gained by buying cheap seeds. Now if you are as far ahead as this it's a good beginning to the year and you will want to keep it up.

Planting. If the weather is dry you can plant some of the trees, shrubs and roses. You will certainly have to make the best of every opportunity. If you're planting any of these please turn to pages 84–87, where I have given detailed instructions.

WORK IN THE GREENHOUSE

Prepare for Seed-sowing. Sowing-time in the greenhouse is getting near. Seed-boxes and pots must be cleaned and got ready for sowing, soil must be mixed ready, but that's a subject we shall be dealing with next month.

There is often a temptation to sow too early and the plants get too large and tend to be starved and overcrowded before it's possible to plant them outside. There's little to be gained by sowing too early, in fact a lot can be lost unless it's possible to maintain a minimum temperature of 50° F.; it's far better to delay sowing for a few weeks until the days lengthen and the sun gains more power.

Chrysanthemum Cuttings.   There should be some good cuttings on the indoor-flowering chrysanthemums and they can be taken this month. Choose the sturdiest growths you can find coming from the base of the plants, they needn't be more than 2 or 3 inches long; cut them with a sharp knife immediately below a leaf-joint, trim off a few of the bottom leaves and they're ready for going in. Put them in pots or boxes, using either pure sand or a mixture of 3 parts of loam, 2 parts of peat and 2 parts of sand.

If they're put in sand only they must be potted into soil as soon as they're rooted, because the sand contains no plant foods to keep them going. If the cuttings are treated with one of the hormone rooting powders you'll find they'll root about a week to ten days earlier than those not treated. If you haven't a frame in the greenhouse to put them in, stand the pots or boxes on the staging, give them one good watering and put some sheets of newspaper over them. This will help to prevent them from flagging; you should never let them flag if you can help it, because once they do they take a long time to recover and take much longer to root. They don't need high temperatures, 45° F. to 55° F. is quite sufficient.

The stools of the outdoor-flowering chrysanthemums can be brought inside from the frame to encourage them to throw up cuttings which we must take next month.

Potting-on.   Schizanthus should be ready for potting-on into 5- or 6-inch pots, also the calceolarias. Stocks and other annuals should be ready for a move on, and the cyclamen sown in May can now go into 3½-inch pots.

Bring in Bulbs.   In the greenhouse we begin to think of spring; bulbs can be brought in from the frames and they won't require a lot of heat to bring them into flower.

A Plan for Flowers through the Year.   If you are keen on growing flowers, as most greenhouse owners are, you will want flowers in the greenhouse throughout the whole twelve months of the year, and so long as you have just sufficient heat to keep out the frost this is easily possible. Most small greenhouses are what we term cool greenhouses, and a wide variety of plants can be grown in a greenhouse such as this. I will give you a list of those I would suggest to keep you going for the whole twelve months.

From January to March you can have the spring-flowering bulbs such as hyacinths, daffodils and tulips, as well as freesias, cinerarias, primulas, and to add richness, camellias, because these do well in a cool greenhouse.

In April, May and June there is a big list to choose from: calceolarias, schizanthus, hydrangeas; and a lot of the hardy and half-hardy annuals flower well in pots at this time too.

For July, August and September I would have the large double-flowering begonias, gloxinias, geraniums, fuchsias, coleus and celosias, and for the last three months of the year, many of those I have already mentioned will continue to flower until the chrysanthemums and cyclamen come into bloom.

If you have a greenhouse, then you should make full use of it. Of those I have mentioned you could include in your seed order cinerarias, primulas (both *obconica* and *malacoides*), freesias because these are stronger when grown from seed than when grown from corms, calceolarias, schizanthus and the various annuals. I like to grow stocks, antirrhinums, salpiglossis and nemesia in pots. Begonias and gloxinias can be grown from seed and will make good flowering plants the same year. We sow some each year, but they need a lot of heat in the early part of the year to start them off and I think it would possibly be better for you to buy the dormant tubers.

Camellias. I mentioned in that list camellias, and I know a lot of people like to grow these but find them difficult. They will of course grow and flower outside. It's true the flowers of some of the earlier varieties do sometimes get caught by frost, but they are well worth planting in the garden.

They don't like lime in the soil but do like plenty of peat and leaf-mould. They will grow and flower well in pots too; they don't need a lot of heat, in fact, if they're given too much the buds soon begin to drop off. A good peaty soil mixture is the ideal, and after they've finished flowering in the greenhouse the pots can be stood outside for the summer; and they like a place where they are partially shaded from the hot sunshine. It is a really delightful flower, almost like wax, and well worth growing.

I find propagating camellias is very fascinating; many people try and many fail, I know. They are very difficult to root from cuttings as you would most other shrubs. The wood is very hard and it's difficult to get the hardwood cuttings to root. The best and certainly the easiest way is to make what we call bud cuttings. To do this a leaf is removed from the stem with a bud attached; it is, in fact, almost like a bud of a rose which is used when budding roses. After selecting a leaf on a branch with a good bud at its base, slide the knife down at the back of the bud and out below it so that you have the leaf and bud with a shield of bark as well. Treat the cut surface at the back of the bud with one of the hormone rooting powders and put it into a pot of moist sand with the leaf itself above. Stand it in the greenhouse, and remember that pure sand gets dry very quickly and it will need watering fairly frequently. The pot can be placed in a poly-thene bag and if the open end of the bag is tied securely it will prevent any loss of moisture, and the leaf-bud will form its roots much sooner. In a matter of weeks roots will be formed and a little time after this the bud will spring into growth, so giving you a new camellia plant. It must, of course, be potted into a peaty soil mixture as soon as the growth begins, because there are little or no plant foods in the pure sand. It's a most fascinating way of propagating and you may like to try it.

Sow Sweet Peas.   In a heated greenhouse you can sow sweet-pea seed. Use the John Innes seed-sowing compost and sow the seeds an inch deep in pots or boxes. Cover the pots or boxes with a sheet of glass and some newspaper, but remove it as soon as the seedlings show through the soil.

FEBRUARY

IN the flower garden any planting of shrubs or trees should be completed before the month is out—and talking of trees, you know it's surprising the number of people who plant forest trees in small gardens. I know how nice it is to take a walk in the country—or take a run in the car—and bring home a fine young seedling sycamore, ash, horse-chestnut, beech or poplar to plant in the garden; these are all very beautiful trees, in a forest or in a field, but not in a small garden; not only do they keep the light from your garden and windows but they also become a nuisance to you—and to your neighbours, with the result that they have to be severely lopped and become an eyesore so long as they remain.

Ornamental Trees. There are many beautiful ornamental trees which will not cause annoyance but will give you pleasure and improve your gardens. I think a few of these are worth mentioning. There are the double-flowering cherries, and make a note of the variety Hisakura, a beautiful rose-pink; the foliage is very attractive throughout the summer and is followed by lovely autumn tints. Then we have the flowering almond, *Prunus Amygdalus*. The flowering Crabs, and make a note of the variety *Pyrus Malus Eleyi*; the flowers are a rich rosy red and the bronze-tinted foliage is very attractive throughout the summer months. The variegated acer, *Acer Negundo,* and the purple-leaved plum *Prunus Pissardii,* to mention only a few.

Prune Winter-flowering Shrubs. Some of the winter-flowering shrubs will soon have completed their flowering period. That's a sign that any pruning that is necessary should be done as soon as possible. The winter-flowering jasmine, *Jasminum nudiflorum,* is usually grown on a wall or trellis and will require the weakest growths thinning out; those that remain should be neatly tied in. The wintersweet, *Chimonanthus fragrans,* the witch hazel, *Hamamelis mollis,* and *Viburnum fragrans* will possibly require

13

thinning or a few of the growths cut back to keep them within bounds.

Divide Herbaceous Plants. Any large clumps of Michaelmas daisies, heleniums, delphiniums, lupins or others will repay you for dividing up. Lift the roots and split them up by pushing into them two garden forks back to back. By pressing the handles together the roots will tear apart. Each clump may make six or more pieces. You know you want only small pieces for replanting, so always choose the outside pieces—they make much the better plants. Prepare the ground well and put in some garden compost or manure, before you replant, because it will possibly be three years before you will need to lift them again.

WORK IN THE GREENHOUSE

Chrysanthemums. In the greenhouse complete the propagating of the indoor-flowering chrysanthemums. Keep the stools of the outdoor-flowering chrysanthemums as near to the glass as possible to encourage sturdy growth. Cuttings put in later in the month will provide you with good plants for planting out in late April and early May. They should be kept under cooler conditions than the cuttings of the indoor-flowering varieties.

Sowing Seeds. Sow the seeds of antirrhinums, salvias, fibrous rooted begonias, lobelia, petunias, verbenas and nicotiana for the summer display, and talking of nicotiana, don't forget a pinch of seed of the variety which you can enjoy in the pipe later in the season. After sowing, cover the boxes or pots with paper until germination takes place and then place them on a shelf as near to the glass as possible.

Geranium Cuttings. The tips of the old geranium stools can be put in and will make good plants for planting out in early June.

Sweet Peas. The sweet peas sown last month should be making good headway; keep them growing under cool conditions, and when they are about 2 to 3 inches high pinch out the small growing tip of each plant to encourage them to throw up a strong growth from the base.

Start Begonia and Gloxinia Tubers. The tubers of begonias and gloxinias can be started into growth.

Potting Composts. Potting composts are certainly improved by sterilizing, but if you have a good maiden loam it isn't essential.

For most plants under glass John Innes potting compost is ideal. This consists of 7 parts of good loam passed through a $\frac{1}{2}$-inch riddle and sterilized, 3 parts of peat and 2 parts of coarse sand. To a bushel of this mixture (the household bucket is approximately a bushel) add 4 oz. of John Innes Base Manure and $\frac{3}{4}$ oz. of ground limestone or chalk.

I may be a bit old-fashioned, but there are still certain plants which I prefer to vary the mixture for and among these are cyclamen, begonias and orchids. I know it isn't possible for the small-greenhouse owner to have elaborate electric or steam sterilizers, but small quantities of soil can be sterilized quite well in a domestic copper. Place the riddled loam in a piece of coarse sacking, bring the four corners together and suspend it over boiling water in the copper by putting a stick across the top, and replace the lid. Place a small potato on the sacking and when this becomes soft the soil will be sufficiently sterilized. The peat and sand do not need sterilizing.

Seed-sowing. And now the seed-sowing in the greenhouse. The type of seeds you sow depends, of course, on the minimum temperature you can maintain. For instance, it's no good sowing tomatoes, begonias or gloxinias if you can't maintain a minimum temperature of 55° F. If you can maintain this, you can sow tomatoes, begonias, gloxinias, salvias, and antirrhinums.

There is, I know, many a small-greenhouse owner who would like to grow the large double begonias, but at the same time feels that he can't afford to buy the tubers, which I must say are rather expensive. There is no reason why he should be without them, they are quite easily grown from seed and if sown this month and kept growing they should make good flowering plants by August. The seed can be bought mixed or in eight separate colours; we sow each year and select the best for growing on. This applies also to the gloxinias which take so many people's eye. Just a word about sowing the begonia seed, it's a very small seed, almost like dust, and if you breathe on it, well, it's gone. Make sure the soil in the pot or box is quite level, otherwise the seed will wash to the hollow places; soak the soil thoroughly and sprinkle a little sand over the surface before sowing. I find the best way is to place the seed on a piece of white paper and allow the seeds to trickle over the one side, keeping the hand moving over the box the whole time. Don't attempt to cover the seed with sand or soil and no further watering is necessary, unless or until the soil begins to show signs of dryness and then allow water to seep up through the drainage rather than water overhead. Cover the pot or box with a sheet of glass and paper and turn the glass each day until you can see the tiny seedlings showing.

Fuchsias.   Now I make no apologies for saying that I am passionately fond of fuchsias; we have some eighty-odd different varieties, but you know I would have difficulty in naming any plant more easy to grow and one which produces such an abundance of flowers over such a long period. They're fine as pot plants, they make good standards, good bedding plants and, if the varieties are carefully chosen, ideal plants for hanging baskets. What is more, they require very little heat to keep them through the winter; in fact, all they need is protection from frost. I often wonder what some people would think if they could see how drastically we treat them at this time of the year. All last year's growth is pruned back to about an inch of the main stem, and all that is left is a straight stem with these inch spurs on it.

We're also just as drastic when repotting them, and while the old plants are still dormant this is an ideal time to do it. The soil round the roots is reasonably dry and there can be little or no food value left in it, so we shake it all off. They're then potted into the smallest-sized pots into which we can get the roots without undue cramping. If they are potted into small pots now it enables us to pot them on into a larger size later on, and that little bit of fresh soil then makes all the difference in the world. We use the John Innes Potting Compost No. 2 for this and future pottings. For this 8 oz. of Base Manure is added to each bushel. After potting, watering must be done very carefully; there isn't a lot of growth at this time of the year and too much water now would make the soil in the pots wet and sour. If the soil is fairly moist as you pot them, then they will not want water for two or perhaps three weeks; all they require is a light spraying over the top on nice days. If you haven't got a fuchsia, then you can buy young plants at this time of the year quite reasonably.

Strike Fuchsia Cuttings.   Cuttings of fuchsias can be put in to provide plants for a hanging basket for the front door or for planting out in the garden.

e Dingle, Quarry Park, the most famous feature of the Shrewsbury Parks, which are superintended by Mr Percy Thrower.

17

Above: Here, I am preparing a pot for potting on, by placing a large piece broken pot over the drainage hole. *Below:* Preparing a box for seed sowing. T drainage slits are covered by pieces of broken pot. A layer of rough peat followed by the compost.

bove: Chrysanthemum cuttings. On the left I am cutting a suitable growth
om the stool. I have prepared the cuttings on the right by trimming them with
sharp knife and removing the lower leaves, and they are now ready for insertion
in sandy compost. *Below:* Taking a bud cutting of a camellia.

Above: Camellia bud cuttings inserted in a mixture of equal parts of sand and peat. When roots form the cuttings can be potted into a peaty mixture. *Below:* Pruning *Viburnum fragrans.* The unpruned bush (left) is developing an upright habit. Some long growths have been removed (right) to induce bushiness.

Above: When dividing a clump of herbaceous perennials I use two forks back to back. Pressing the handles together will tear the clumps apart. *Below:* Taking fuchsia cuttings. I take young shoots 3 to 4 inches long from the parent plant, trim them below a joint and insert them in sandy compost.

Above: Pruning. I prune my bush roses to within 5 or 6 inches of the old wood (left). On the right a purple buddleia which flowers on the new wood has been cut back, removing the previous year's growth. *Below:* Damping down. Spraying water on the staging helps to maintain a humid atmosphere.

Above: Sowing seeds of hardy annuals broadcast. I sow these very thinly in a sunny bed, and rake them in (below left). *Below:* On the right a chrysanthemum plant, properly hardened off, is being planted out. Note the stake already in position, and the use of the trowel for firming.

23

Above: The newly planted chrysanthemum is tied to its stake immediately to prevent any damage by wind. Note the label. If the ground is wet use a board to stand or kneel on. *Below:* Planting out gladioli corms. A handful of sand is placed in the hole before planting.

MARCH

DON'T you get a thrill when you see the tiny green tips showing on the hedges, shrubs and trees? I do, and I always think the spring is the most interesting season of the year, at any rate it is to the gardener. At this time of year I like to take a walk round to see how many flowers I can find, apart from the spring bulbs; the purple *Daphne Mezereum* is a picture, and it has such a beautiful scent; *Viburnum fragrans* often still has a nice show of its pinky-white blossom, it flowers exceptionally well with me. *Erica carnea* and its varieties are in flower, the witch hazel, *Hamamelis mollis* often still shows its yellow flowers as does the winter jasmine, *Jasminum nudiflorum,* on the wall. *Garrya elliptica* looks beautiful with its elegant green catkins. There are sometimes a few brave flowers on the winter-flowering pansies and polyanthus, and here and there a touch of flower on the aubrieta and other rock plants.

Pruning Bush Roses.   In the flower garden the bush roses will want pruning and the latter part of the month is the correct time. To be successful in producing good roses you must be severe, they must be cut back hard, and apart from anything else it prolongs the life of the bushes, it keeps them young. All the growth produced last year should be cut back to within four or five buds of the old wood; that means that you would leave approximately 5 or 6 inches of last year's growth. I remember that once a friend of mine who had planted a new rose bed asked my advice on pruning. When I called in to see his roses his wife was out, and after the pruning was done he was horrified to see stumps not more than 5 or 6 inches above the ground. I believe that when his wife came back he was 'on the carpet', but he had some jolly fine roses during the summer.

Shrub Pruning.   Some of the summer-flowering shrubs want pruning too. Among these are the purple buddleias, ceanothus and tamarix, shrubs which flower on the current year's growth.

Last year's growth should be cut back hard to within 2 or 3 inches of the old wood.

If you have a clematis on the wall, that will want pruning back to a good strong bud too. We have a dark purple variety; the buds are very prominent and, of course, it is necessary to sacrifice quite a few of them. I bring mine down to about 5 or 6 feet and select the best and strongest growths to leave.

Hydrangea paniculata will want pruning hard back too, but please don't let me confuse you. I don't mean the ordinary hydrangeas which are often grown in pots or under the wall of a house (that is *H. Hortensia*, and shouldn't be pruned at this time of year). *H. paniculata* is a large white-flowering variety and flowers on long growths of the current year's wood.

Now I think that's all you'll want me to name for now. If you study your shrubs carefully you can't go wrong, as those which flower on the young growths you prune in spring, those that flower on growths produced the previous year you prune after flowering.

WORK IN THE GREENHOUSE

Chrysanthemums. In the greenhouse the chrysanthemums mustn't be neglected, as any neglect at this time of the year will reflect on the plants for the remainder of the season. Keep them up to the light as much as you can and give them all the air possible, they don't want high temperatures. Indoor chrysanthemums should be nicely rooted in $3\frac{1}{2}$-inch pots, and will be ready for their next move into 5-inch pots towards the end of the month. The early-flowering chrysanthemums should be rooting very nicely too, and will want moving from the frame very soon. A day or two out of the propagating frame and then they can be transferred to a cold frame and given protection only on frosty nights.

Seed-sowing. There's more seed-sowing to do this month, and among the most important are nicotiana, the flowering tobacco, petunias, lobelias, stocks, asters, zinnias, if these were not sown last month. Now, a lot of people admire zinnias but say they're never successful with them. They shouldn't be difficult; they don't like being disturbed too much, so what we do is sow the seed directly into pots and not in boxes. Sow two or three seeds on the top of each 3½-inch pot, and when the seeds germinate select the strongest plant and pull out the remainder. Always water the pots very carefully, err on the dry side rather than the other way, give them plenty of air and light and never subject them to high temperatures. Harden them off and plant out at the end of May in a sunny place.

Greenhouse Ventilation. When the sun comes out the temperature in the greenhouse rises very quickly. This, of course, means that growth is being speeded up, and in most cases we don't want it to be speeded up too much. As the temperature rises the ventilators must be opened, a little at a time to begin with and always on the sheltered side of the house first to avoid cold draughts; then they should be closed before the sun goes down so that you are conserving and making full use of the sun's heat. You know, it is far better and cheaper than all the heat from hot-water pipes or electricity.

If you're away at business all day then I know it is very difficult, but I'm sure the wife would be quite willing to help you with this. Proper ventilation and keeping the correct temperature is so essential at this time of the year; I would go so far as to say more important than at any other time. Generally speaking I think it could be said, don't aim at too high a temperature and avoid a rapid rise or fall in temperature at all times.

Damping Down. And now what about the atmosphere in the greenhouse? I expect you know as well as I that a dry atmosphere is not what we could call a growing one. When a gardener walks into a greenhouse he likes to feel a rather close, humid atmosphere, and straight away he'll say 'Ah, you can almost feel the plants growing'. If the air in the greenhouse is kept too dry it does, of course, encourage red-spider mite, thrips and other insect pests. This can be avoided and that growing atmosphere maintained if, when the temperature begins to rise, the paths and stagings, but not necessarily the plants, are sprayed with water; in fact when the sun is shining at this time of year I never like to see the floor of the greenhouse dry, and it is an advantage to spray water underneath the staging too.

Jobs in the Heated Greenhouse. If you have a greenhouse or frame then there are a whole host of jobs that can be done, and welcome ones too, when the weather is not too good. But I must keep my remarks for the unheated greenhouse separate from those for the heated house, because the difference in night temperature, and often day temperature, will be considerable.

We'll take the heated ones first, and whether they're heated by hot-water pipes, electricity or a paraffin lamp doesn't matter very much, so long as it is possible to keep the minimum night temperature around about 45° F.

There are the cuttings of the outdoor-flowering chrysanthemums to take, and the dahlia tubers to place in peat on the stagings if you want to take cuttings of these. Cuttings of coleus, fuchsias, geraniums, begonias, and verbenas can be put in too.

Jobs in the Unheated Greenhouse.   Now a word about the unheated house or frame, and if you have one I know you realize you've got to be much later with things generally. You've got to rely on the outside temperature and the sun heat and, as I said earlier on, make full use of what sun heat there is. Be content with sowing such flower seeds as sweet peas, antirrhinums, asters, stocks, alyssum and any of those which we class as hardy annuals. The majority of these you will sow in boxes or pots by scattering the seed over a level soil surface, but there are just one or two points I want to make. These may seem to you unnecessary if you've been sowing your own seeds for years, but there are always people doing it, possibly for the first time.

Firstly, the boxes or pots should be clean and there must be plenty of drainage. All boxes should have holes or spaces in the bottom, so that the water can drain away freely. At the bottom of the pots put some pieces of broken pot or old clinker ash to make sure the seedlings get good drainage, then a good seed soil mixture, such as John Innes standard seed-sowing compost, which has, apart from loam and peat, plenty of coarse sand or grit to keep the soil open and so further assist with the drainage. You can buy the seed compost already mixed up. Fill the pots or boxes and make the soil moderately firm, and make sure when you've finished that the soil surface is perfectly level. Water before you sow the seed so that the whole bulk of soil is thoroughly soaked. However small the seeds are sow them very thinly and only just cover them with fine soil.

APRIL

APART from the bad weather, we often get nice spells of warm sunshine in April, too, and we are often tempted to begin planting for the summer display. No doubt, as usual, we shall see on the market this month those boxes of rather thin, drawn-up half-hardy annuals, such as African and French marigolds, *Phlox Drummondii*, lobelia and zinnias, as well as geraniums and salvias and many of the more tender plants, but don't be tempted to buy just yet or you may find you'll have to buy again next month; the second half of May is plenty soon enough for planting all these types of plants. There should be plenty of bedding plants for everybody later next month. I think the important thing is this, what sort of plants are you going to buy? Those which have been too close together in the boxes and have got thin and drawn, those that are showing their flowers, or those dark green, sturdy plants which tell you right away that when you've planted them they'll grow and make a really colourful show for you? You be guided by me, don't buy them if they're thin and drawn, and with the exception of possibly geraniums, salvias and fuchsias, don't buy them if they're coming into flower. The best example I can quote is the stocks; if these are showing their flower-buds when they're planted they'll never make good plants, they'll just send up that one little flower-spike and then finish.

Sowing Hardy Annuals. In the seed catalogues you will find a large number of flowers marked H.A., meaning that they're hardy annuals, and all flowers so marked can be sown in the open ground, preferably where they are to flower, and they will give you a good display of colour from June right through until the frosts come in the autumn. This month and early next, when the soil is in good condition, is an ideal time for sowing, and you need only a small packet of each kind or variety. They want sowing very thinly, a pinch of seed of any of them should produce quite a reasonable group. By careful sowing you can sow a border 30 feet by 6 feet for about six shillings and have a very attractive summer display.

Now what are the main requirements of the hardy annuals? Firstly, they are sun-loving plants, so require a position in the sun as much as possible. They don't want a soil which is too rich but one that has been well worked and reasonably good, a little garden compost or manure worked into the soil will help them over a dry period, and a little general fertilizer, about an ounce to the square yard raked into the surface, should provide them with all they will require. Before sowing make the soil in the bed or border firm by treading and then rake the surface down as fine as you can. Next, with a pointed stick in the fine soil you can mark the border off into irregular pockets or patches; don't make the groups too small, those at the back of the border could be 3 or more feet across each way and those at the front about 2 feet each way.

On the seed-packets there should be the height and colour, put this on the label as well as the name, as that's very important. You can then place the labels in the various pockets or groups and move them about to where you think best before sowing, and this is where you invite the wife to come in with her advice, otherwise it's almost a certainty that your arrangement and colour-scheming will be criticized.

When you've sorted it out between yourselves the sowing can commence. Scatter the seed very thinly over the areas you have marked out, and I mean thinly, as you know most of these plants will require to be 9 to 12 or more inches apart, then lightly rake the seeds into the surface with a small rake. With some of the larger seeds, such as the annual lupins, you may find it easier to push the individual seeds in with the finger; the larger the seeds the more covering they will require. If you think the sparrows or other birds may be troublesome by dust-bathing in the fine soil and disturbing the seeds, thread a little black cotton from stick to stick, about 6 inches above the border and then it can be left until the seedlings are large enough for thinning, but that's a subject I shall deal with later.

There are many of the hardy annuals I would like to mention, but no doubt you have your own particular favourites, but here are six which I consider worthy of being included in any border —annual anchusa, annual chrysanthemum, calliopsis, linaria, eschscholtzia (California poppy) and bartonia.

Top-dressing Alpines. If you have alpines in the garden it's an opportune time to clean up round them, just stirring the soil to freshen it, and a top-dressing of fresh soil will do them a world of good.

A mixture of soil and peat with a little bonemeal or meat-and bonemeal added makes a good top-dressing, not only for alpines but for other plants in the garden too. It needs to be spread round the plants about half an inch deep. As the plants begin to grow in the spring it's a good time for feeding, particularly if you use the slower-acting organic manures, such as bonemeal, steamed bone flour, hoof and horn meal or the meat and bone. There is, on the market, a by-product known as 'skin and bone meal' with added magnesium, and it's a very reasonable price compared with other organic fertilizers. I have used it and found it very good.

How to Use Manures. The important thing when using any manures such as these, in fact any bag manures, is to keep them away from the stems of the plants: far too much damage is done every year by putting concentrated manures too close to the stems and leaves of plants. They should be sprinkled on the surface round the plants, and lightly stirred in. The roots will find them, or at least the soluble plant foods from them, and you can rest assured they won't be wasted. When sowing seeds too, it's as well to remember that the seeds should not come into direct contact with manure. For instance, it's wrong to scatter fertilizers along the drills before sowing seeds. If there should be little or no rain to wash it into the soil the young seedlings will be scorched.

Plant out Sweet Peas. We can plant out our sweet peas so long as they are well hardened off. You know, I like growing them in double rows on single stems, you get the finer flowers and the longer stem; I know it means a lot of tying and disbudding, but that's a job the wife should be pleased to do, and you will be able to go round to see your pals with that fine spray with six or more flowers on. Put the plants in a foot apart each way in the double rows and don't disturb the roots any more than you can help, plant them firmly, and if the soil is inclined to be dry give them a good watering in, put a stake or cane to each plant, preferably 8 to 10 feet in height, and select the strongest growth from the base of each plant to train up.

Plant out Chrysanthemums. The outdoor chrysanthemums should be ready for planting out after the middle of the month. Make sure they are well hardened off too, they appreciate a piece of well-prepared ground that has had plenty of good manure, and make it firm before planting. Don't forget that you want room to work between them for tying, disbudding, feeding, hoeing and cutting, etc., so give them at least 2 feet apart each way. I always think it a good plan to put the stakes in first and plant to the stakes and tie in immediately. In any case, they should be given support as soon as they're planted. It's very disappointing to plant out those fine plants you have tended so carefully, and next morning look out of the window and find the wind has broken a number of them off. If the soil is dry, water them in thoroughly, it helps to settle the plants in and give them a good start.

Dividing Outdoor Chrysanthemums. You know, when we talk of taking chrysanthemum cuttings, potting them and putting them in the frame, we're apt to forget the person without either a greenhouse or a frame. How does he manage? He, no doubt, leaves them out all winter, protected either with some straw or cloches over them. At this time of the year they're beginning to send up their new growths. Round about the middle of the month the roots can be lifted and all the soil shaken off, each growth can then be pulled away and you'll find they've no doubt formed root on the part of the stem which was underground. Each shoot like this can be planted out in the normal way and they will make reasonably good plants so long as they're watered and looked after until they get established.

Thinning Herbaceous Plants. It will pay to spend a little time among the herbaceous plants; if the clumps of phlox, delphiniums, Michaelmas daisies, heleniums, solidago, lupins, etc., haven't been divided for a year or two they will be throwing up a large number of growths. Thin these growths down to not more than five or eight on each clump, the spikes will be stronger and the individual flowers will be finer. If there are any of these plants which you wish to propagate take the growths off well below ground-level and put them in a cold frame in a sandy mixture and keep them

Pricking off cineraria seedlings. Before the seedlings become too crowded in the pans I am pricking them off into other boxes of John Innes potting compost. I handle them with great care, lifting them with a label as above and spacing them out well as shown below.

Greenfly breed rapidly in the spring on the young growths of roses and will soon cripple and spoil the early blooms. I spray my rose bushes regularly with nicotine, BHC, pyrethrum or derris. I spray forcibly, using a syringe with a fine jet and making sure that I spray under the leaves as well.

Here, I am preparing a double row of canes, up which sweet peas will be grown cordon fashion. I remove the tendrils to prevent them twining themselves round the flower stems. But if that is done you have to tie the stems to the canes as in the photograph below.

Above: Removing the side shoots of sweet peas to throw all the vigour into the cordon stem. When the plant reaches the top of the cane it is laid along the bottom of the row and trained up a cane further along. *Below:* I stake tall-growing annuals at an early stage. As they grow they will hide the stakes.

close; they will root quite easily and provide you with good plants for the following season.

Gladioli. And now the gladioli. I don't think there is any plant that gives a larger flower-spike of such beautiful flowers than the gladiolus, and what a wonderful range of colours to choose from. For indoor decoration the smaller-growing primulinus types are the best. You know, the gladiolus is a really good buy at the present time, I see they're anything from ten to twenty-five shillings a hundred, and you couldn't call that expensive (unless, of course, you want to go in for the newer up-to-date varieties), and with care they will continue to flower for you year after year. Some varieties flower earlier than others, so by having a mixture you prolong the flowering period and you can have the gladioli in flower from July to November.

These, too, like a fairly rich soil because, apart from producing you some fine blooms this year, they have the job of building up a good corm for next year. They want to be planted about 4 inches deep, and a handful of sand placed in the hole before you put in the corm provides a nice rooting medium for them to start in. In the Midlands it is quite safe to plant the dormant corms after the middle of the month, and if you didn't have them in your garden last year I certainly would do this time.

Evergreens. Most people like to have a few evergreens in their garden, either in groups to themselves or planted among the deciduous shrubs so that there's some green foliage in the garden throughout the whole of the year. They're often planted as a windbreak to shelter the house, or somewhere in the garden where it's nice to sit out, or to shelter some other tender plants or shrubs. They could, of course, be used to prevent the neighbours looking over, or to provide privacy from the road. I think that care should be taken not to overplant, particularly with the darker types of evergreen; they can give the garden a very heavy, dark appearance.

There is, of course, a whole list to choose from, and the better-known ones include holly, yew, cupressus, privet, box and laurel, and on soils that are free from lime we must include the rhododendron. The first mentioned can be had in the golden and variegated forms, and they're most attractive when planted with other shrubs, they relieve that dark, heavy green. There's the golden privet, golden cupressus and yew, variegated holly and laurel, or perhaps we had better give it its proper name, *Aucuba japonica variegata*. I mention evergreens because April is the ideal month for planting these, they don't take kindly to being moved during the winter. During this month the roots are very active and quickly find their way into the new soil. If the weather is inclined to be dry after planting they'll get established much more quickly if you can water them once or twice.

Hedges. Those people with new gardens, and possibly some with established gardens too, will be faced with the problem of a boundary fence or a boundary hedge; for preference give me a hedge every time. I'm quite certain the cost of maintenance is much less in the long run, and apart from that, a hedge fits in with the garden much better than a wooden fence. A wire fence provides no privacy or shelter whatsoever, and looks too much like a chicken-run or pig-pen.

The next thing is, what kind of a hedge are you going to choose? We might for a moment discuss the more popular types of hedge plants, and I suppose the first that comes to most people's mind is privet. It is true there are few shrubs which will make a good hedge in quicker time than privet, but I think that's about the only thing in its favour. It certainly wouldn't be my choice, because the privet is a very hungry plant and forms a lot of fibrous root near the surface; apart from this, to keep a privet hedge looking tidy and nice it needs clipping four or five times a year.

The quickthorn, or perhaps you may know it as the hawthorn, is not, of course, evergreen, and if you decide on this one it will have to be planted during the first week or so. Once established it is fairly fast growing and certainly makes a good boundary hedge, one that will prevent anyone pushing through it. The plants are reasonably cheap, and clipping once or twice a year is enough to keep the hedge looking as it should. While the privet can be planted in a single row, about $1\frac{1}{2}$ to 2 feet apart, the quick-thorn will need to be planted in a double row 1 foot apart each way, and you can allow approximately five to the yard.

Both the *Cupressus Lawsoniana* and the *Thuya Lobbii* make a very attractive evergreen hedge. They are more expensive to buy, but not exactly slow growing. Once established a clipping once a year in July is all that's needed to keep them in good shape. These are best planted in a single row 2 or 3 feet apart during this month.

Both holly and yew make good hedges, but they're rather slow, so is box, and I'm quite certain that laurel should never be used as a hedge plant, it makes a good screen, but the foliage is badly disfigured as soon as it comes to clipping. Where it has been planted as a hedge then each shoot should be cut back with the sécateurs: never use the shears on a laurel hedge.

Beech is attractive because it holds those golden-brown leaves all winter, but the trouble is it sheds them in the spring when everywhere is clean and tidy. My choice would be either quick-thorn or the *Cupressus Lawsoniana*.

WORK IN THE GREENHOUSE

Pricking out Seedlings. We shall be busy in the greenhouse this month pricking out the various seedlings, a job which must be tackled before the plants get overcrowded in the seed-boxes. It is at this stage that some growers find difficulty with damping off, particularly with asters, antirrhinums, stocks, petunias and others. Well, to help to overcome this, firstly handle the young plants with great care and for the first watering of the boxes use a solution of Cheshunt Compound, according to the makers' instructions; it will greatly reduce the amount of losses. Shade the boxes from the bright sunshine for a few days, and as soon as you see the young plants beginning to establish themselves give them all the ventilation you can on nice days; don't coddle them, they want to be kept sturdy.

MAY

MAY is, I suppose, one of the gardener's busiest months. There will be a hundred and one jobs staring us in the face.

Stopping Early Chrysanthemums. Early-flowering chrysanthemums will require stopping after the middle of May, or not later than the first week in June, and it's most essential that the plants should be well established and making good growth when this is done or it will give them a severe check, which must be avoided if we are to be successful. Perhaps I should explain the term 'stopping'—by this I mean pinching out the young growing tip of each growth to encourage the plants to break or send up a number of growths, preferably six or eight, which will each provide you with a fine bloom in time for your local show.

Sweet Peas. The sweet peas should be making good growth, so keep them carefully tied in and remove the side-shoots as they appear at each leaf joint; I also like to remove the tendrils from the ends of the leaves—you know what I mean: those curly things which twine themselves round everything they come into contact with—otherwise they fasten themselves round the flower stems with the result that the stems are anything but straight. Keep them watered during dry spells and give them occasional feeds with liquid manure or a good general fertilizer and remember, the golden rule is 'little and often', and don't allow the fertilizer to come into contact with the stems.

Thinning Annuals. The hardy annuals now require thinning and you have to be really hard hearted when you begin this operation; don't be afraid to pull a large number of the small plants out. After thinning the remaining plants should not be closer than 9 to 12 inches, and the taller-growing varieties not less than 18 inches apart.

Summer Bedding. During the second half of the month you will see the gardeners in your public parks busy with the summer bedding, and you can take it for granted that it is time you started yours. All the half-hardy annuals such as zinnias and nemesia as well as geraniums and salvias can safely be planted out. Space will not allow for me to go into details of colour and bedding schemes, but I feel sure you'll enjoy working out your own schemes: it makes it so much more interesting. One word of advice I would offer and that is, don't overcrowd the plants in the beds and borders, give them plenty of room to grow and develop, they will give you a much longer service, and make sure every plant is well firmed after planting.

Roses. We must watch the young growths on the roses for greenfly, because they breed rapidly at this time of the year and will soon cripple and spoil the early roses which we look forward to next month.

Supporting Herbaceous Plants. We must think about putting supports to the plants on the herbaceous border. They'll need support against the strong winds and to give the border that neat and orderly appearance.

I find the best way of supporting the plants is with last year's pea sticks if you haven't used them for lighting the fire. You know approximately to what height most of your plants will grow, if you don't you can soon find it in the nurseryman's catalogue. Push the sticks well into the ground, round and a few inches away from the clumps so as not to damage the roots. The plants will grow up and through the sticks, they don't look unsightly and, what's more, they don't give that bundled-up appearance which often happens when the plants are tied to a stake or cane. If you haven't got pea sticks and you have to use canes, just loop the twine loosely round them so that the growths are not drawn in together. All you put the support there for is to prevent them falling over or being damaged by strong winds.

After-care of Bulbs. When the daffodils and tulips have finished flowering don't lift them from the beds and cast them aside, the bulbs will not have completed their growth, and with a little care they will flower again next spring. Heel them in on a spare piece of the garden where the tops can die down gradually. You can then lift them and put them away until planting time comes round again in the autumn.

Hanging Baskets. And now what about a nice hanging basket for the front door? Far too often we see baskets of about 8 to 10 inches in diameter and only a few inches deep; that's not big enough, I like to see a basket which begins flowering in June and continues until late September, and that's within the reach of everyone if you use a large enough basket, and give it the proper care and attention during the summer. Choose a basket not less than 12 inches in diameter and at least 6 inches in depth; this will hold sufficient soil to maintain throughout the summer from four to twelve plants according to the kind you use.

Of course, it's not all plants which are suitable for use in hanging baskets, so let's see what we have to choose from. There are fuchsias, ivy-leaved geraniums, petunias, trailing lobelia, nasturtiums, particularly the double Golden Gleam and its hybrids, verbenas, ageratum, tagetes, some of the dwarfer-growing hardy annuals, and of course the variegated nepeta.

And now to set about making up the basket. First of all line it with some nice green moss; next we want some good soil, because we must remember the plants have only a restricted root space. The best soil to use would be some good loam, a little peat and sand, some well-decayed manure or compost, and a good handful of bone flour to each bucketful of soil, all well mixed together. Next, half fill the basket with soil and press it in as firmly as you can with the hands, put in a little more soil and the basket is ready for the plants. If you use the ivy-leaved geraniums and trailing lobelia, which is a very nice combination, push some of the lobelia through the sides of the basket and then three or four geraniums round the top interplanted with more lobelia; fill the basket to the top with soil and press down firmly again, and finish off saucer-like to hold the water.

There are some beautiful varieties of fuchsias well suited for the hanging basket; you know, I think they're the most graceful of all and the varieties I would choose are Cascade, Marinka, Falling Stars, Trailing Queen and Mrs Marshall. If you use any of these varieties three or four would be ample, and it's not necessary to use lobelia or any other plants with them.

When the making up is finished give the basket a thorough soaking, and when you hang it outside towards the end of the month or early in June, it will require a good watering every day and a little fertilizer, a good dessertspoonful mixed in a gallon of water once a week, but never do this when the basket is dry, water it well first and then water it again with the fertilizer.

Window-boxes. And now the window-box. For this we have a larger variety of plants to choose from. Apart from those mentioned for the hanging basket there are the salvias, geraniums, alyssum, calceolarias and a host of others. Make sure the box is secure on the window sill and that you have drainage holes in the bottom. I have often noticed that where window-boxes and tubs are used there is a tendency to paint them in bright colours; to my idea that's wrong—the boxes or tubs should not be made too prominent, they're provided only to hold soil for the plants to grow in, it's the plants and flowers that want to be conspicuous; surely a dull green paint is sufficient.

Put a few stones or pieces of broken pot in the bottom of the box and fill it with some good soil. You can have some good fun in arranging your plants and colours and I'm sure it would be exciting to have a better window-box than the person next door. In the early stages a good watering every few days should be sufficient, and if it's a nice sunny window, when the plants get established, they will want water every day, and fertilizer once a week.

WORK IN THE GREENHOUSE AND FRAME

Sow Cyclamen Seeds. I like to sow cyclamen this month, to allow approximately eighteen months from sowing to flowering, and I feel sure that if they're grown cool throughout they make much better plants than those sown later and grown in high temperatures. You know, the cyclamen is one of our best winter-flowering plants, it begins flowering in November and continues through to Easter. Make up a mixture of soil which includes plenty of sharp sand and space the seeds out about an inch apart. Cover the seeds with about a quarter of an inch of soil and put the pots in a cold frame, preferably under a north wall.

Primula obconica, cinerarias and calceolarias can also be sown and put in the same frame.

JUNE

A GARDENER must always look ahead, and it's time that we began thinking about preparations for next spring.

Sow Seeds of Spring Bedding Plants. Wallflowers, cheiranthus, (the Siberian wallflowers), myosotis, or perhaps we had better speak of it as forget-me-not, and the white, red and pink double daisies can all be sown this month; they don't need to be put in a frame and can be sown in the open garden. I think they're better sown in drills than sown broadcast: it all adds to the neat and tidy apearance of the garden and it's so much easier to cover the seeds. All seeds require covering at this time of the year; other-wise, with the rapid drying of the surface soil, germination will be very irregular. Make the drills about ½ inch deep and 9 inches apart, just so that you can get the hoe between them to keep down the weeds. Sow the seed thinly along the drills and push the soil back with the feet, then very lightly rake over the bed to give it a neat finish; draw the rake the same way as the drills and you won't pull the seed out of the rows. If the soil is very dry it's a good plan to water along the drills before you sow, it will hasten germination.

It might be worth mentioning a few varieties. Of the forget-me-nots I think the dwarf strain of Royal Blue is the best, it's a very compact grower; and among the best of the wallflowers are Orange Bedder, Golden Bedder, Fire King, Primrose Bedder and Scarlet Emperor, they're all of a good habit. I purposely leave out Blood Red and Vulcan because there are some very poor strains on the market at the present time, and I don't like the variety Eastern Queen, it is a very dull colour for the spring and doesn't show up well against those I've already mentioned. Among the daisies I think the best is Red Quilled. A lot of people like the daisies, to look at; I do, but I always try to avoid planting them near the grass, they produce seed very freely and it isn't long before you see hundreds of daisy seedlings coming up in the lawn.

bove: I find that last year's pea sticks are very useful for supporting herbaceous *l*ants. Push them well into the ground round the clumps and a few inches away *s* I am doing here. *Below:* Heel your daffodil and tulip bulbs in on a spare piece of ground where the tops can die down naturally.

Hanging baskets. *Above:* Line a deep basket with moss. Half fill it with a properl[y] made up soil mixture such as I have described in the text. Firm the soil and ad[d] a little more and then plant it up. Among the plants you can use are fuchsia[s] lobelias, geraniums or, as below, begonias.

Window boxes. *Above:* Before putting your window box in position nail small blocks of wood at the corners. This will enable you to have a drip tray underneath to catch the surplus moisture. Note the drainage holes. *Below:* Use a trowel for planting and don't plant too closely.

Cyclamen. *Above:* Prepare a compost containing plenty of sharp sand fo cyclamen seed, and after you have filled the pan firm the compost as I am doin here. *Below:* I sow the seeds singly, spacing them about an inch apart, an covering them with about a quarter of an inch of soil.

Cyclamen. *Above:* After sowing I cover the pans with a sheet of glass and newspaper (left) and place them in a cold frame. When the seeds have germinated and formed their first leaves they can be carefully pricked off (right) into boxes of John Innes compost, spacing them out as I am doing below.

Above left: After aubrieta has finished flowering I cut back some of the old flowered growths. *Above right:* I stake my dahlias using three canes round the plant, and tying the plant in with soft twine as I am doing below (left). I obtain large blooms by removing side buds as on the right.

50

Repotting old cyclamen corms. When the new growth begins late in the summer take the plant out of its pot and remove some of the old compost from round the corm (above). Then I repot, using fresh compost, in a slightly larger pot, not forgetting the drainage material.

Above: Final potting of cyclamen. I prepare the pots, place the plant in the centre and sift compost all round it, firming it as I go along. *Below:* Here, I am preparing for the final potting of a chrysanthemum. I place drainage crocks in the bottom of the pot, followed by a good layer of rough material.

Winter-flowering Pansies. I think a place should be found in every garden for the winter-flowering pansies; they're very hardy, they stand the winter well; whenever we get a mild spell during the winter it's possible to find a few flowers on them and they make a fine display during March, April and May; in fact, I always loathe pulling them up at the end of May as they're still full of flower. I can quite imagine that if they were in some gardens the wife would be saying, 'You're not going to disturb that bed', and if she does, well, what can you do? They will, however, continue flowering during most of the summer, so there will be no need to slip out early one morning and pull them up. There are a number of varieties; the best of the blues are Blue Boy and Celestial Queen; Helios is a good rich yellow and North Pole is an excellent pure white.

Sow the seed in boxes and put them in the frame, when they're large enough to handle they can be pricked out in the garden and then transferred to their flowering quarters in October or early November. The greenfly is very fond of them, so keep an eye on them and if you see the leaves beginning to curl, spray the plants thoroughly with a nicotine spray.

Treatment of Rock Plants after Flowering. Well, the aubrieta, many of the saxifragas, the phlox, rock roses and many others will soon have finished flowering for this year and will be making their new growth for next spring flowering. Now, don't neglect the poor things; as soon as the flowers have gone you can cut back a lot of the more straggly growths, top-dress round them with a little fresh soil, a mixture of loam, peat, sand and a little bone-meal and see that they don't suffer for the want of water throughout the summer; they will repay you a hundred times over next spring.

Cuttings of Rock Plants. You have, perhaps, some favourites that you will want to increase, if that's so, now is the time to begin thinking about it. Watch the plants carefully and when you see the new young growths coming from the base of the plants that's the time to take the cuttings; that's the material you want and you'll find they will root reasonably easy. Cut off a few of these young growths, below the soil if possible, with a sharp knife, put them in pots in a mixture of 2 parts of loam, 1 part of peat and 1 part of sharp sand, preferably round the sides of the pots; label the pots and plunge them up to the rim in sand, in a cold frame. Give them a good watering, keep the frame closed and cover the glass with sacking on bright days. They will tell you when they're beginning to root, you will see them looking a brighter green and beginning to make new growth; you can then ventilate the frame freely and reduce the shading gradually and after a time leave it off altogether; these will make you nice flowering plants for next spring and will all be true to type and colour, which is most important.

Dividing Primulas. The primulas, such as *P.* Wanda, *rosea*, Julia, *denticulata* and *P. Auricula* are best divided. You will notice that the plants have made several crowns; lift them carefully and divide them up into as many as you require, and plant them in a nice, cool, shady place and keep them watered. They will make good flowering plants and can go back on to the rock garden in the autumn.

Dahlias. Of the many summer-flowering plants the dahlia is a great favourite, and it's not to be wondered at when you realize how well it grows and flowers in almost any kind of soil, and the continual display of colour it will provide from June right through until the frosts come in the autumn. Also, of course, with a little care, the tubers can be kept from year to year, thus saving the expense of buying afresh each spring.

There are a number of different types of dahlias and we gardeners know them as dwarf bedders, the singles and doubles of various colours which grow $1\frac{1}{2}$ to 2 feet high and flower extremely freely; this is probably the most popular type of all.

The pompom dahlias, or pompon as they should be correctly called, which vary in height up to 4 feet, are becoming more and more popular. Very prim and proper, neat little flowers, all double and honey-combed in a very orderly manner, they include many beautiful shades and are useful for making up small bowls.

The Charm dahlias are the semi-doubles which form good stems and are well suited for arrangement in bowls and vases.

The cactus and semi-cactus, with neat, quilled, spiky-looking flowers, make a fine display in the garden, and are also useful for indoor decoration.

The decorative dahlias include the medium-sized through to the very large flowers, and apart from the exhibition table, the very large ones are of little value for indoor decoration. They make a very attractive and interesting display in the garden and I find that a large number of people are thrilled with these large (what I would term 'cabbage-like') flowers in July, August and September.

And now what about varieties? We shall be seeing many of the older and the newer varieties at the various shows throughout the summer and autumn, and shall be able to choose for ourselves, but I think it would be well worth while mentioning just a few. For this purpose we will divide them into two main groups, the first for making a colourful display in the smaller beds and borders round the house, and the second for the larger borders, and for cutting for indoor decoration.

Coltness Gem, the single bright scarlet bedding variety, is, no doubt, the most widely known, but I think it has now been superseded by better varieties. Maureen Creighton, of recent introduction, is a very beautiful double scarlet. Princess Marie José is a very nice single pink, and a good single yellow is Northern Gold. You know, apart from calceolarias and marigolds there are not many good yellows among the summer bedding plants, so we often have to fall back on the yellow dahlias, and I think Northern Gold is the best.

Now for the second group, and in my estimation the first of these is the old favourite Bishop of Llandaff, a bright crimson semi-double with dark bronze foliage, one that is continually finding its way into the decorative classes at the summer shows. Another is Andreas Orange, a bright orange semi-cactus. Baby Royal, an old favourite, I purposely leave out, because the stock generally seems to be deteriorating. Girlie is a beautiful little pale mauve pompon; New Vision is a very fine shell-pink cactus, and of the very large ones I like Jane Cowl, a buff shaded with orange.

You have, no doubt, or at least you should have by this time, planted your dahlias and the first flowers will be showing. I find that generally it is not appreciated how much room a dahlia requires, it is our most economical bedding plant owing to the space it is necessary to leave between the plants. The bedding varieties should not be planted closer than 1½ feet and the larger ones anything from 2 to 4 feet apart each way, so, you see, you don't need many to fill the average-sized bed or border.

And now a word about the attention during the growing season. They do need attention, you know, if they are to give of their best, the taller-growing varieties will need support against strong winds, either by one strong cane at the back of the plant and the growths loosely looped to it, or three canes round the plant and neatly strung round with green twine, which is much more satisfactory. They like plenty of water whenever the weather is dry, and an occasional dusting round the plants with a good fertilizer; they will repay you a hundred times over for that extra little attention. Instead of putting the lawn mowings on your compost heap, or throwing them away, spread them round your dahlias, it will form a good mulch and will greatly reduce the amount of watering.

And, as a final word, keep all the dead flowers cut off, it all adds to the neat and tidy appearance of the garden, and your dahlias will flower over a much longer period and the individual flowers will be finer.

WORK IN THE GREENHOUSE AND FRAME

Pot-on Cyclamen.   The cyclamen should be ready for their final pots before the end of the month, and when you pot them see that the top of the corm is just above the level of the soil. I like to keep it below the soil until the final potting, and for the final potting 5- or 6-inch pots are plenty large enough.

Prick out Primulas.   The *Primula obconica* seedlings will be ready for pricking out into other boxes or potting off into small pots.

Pot-on Chrysanthemums.   If the chrysanthemums are not in their final pots, well, it's a job that must be done before the middle of the month; 8½-inch pots will be plenty large enough. Ram the soil firmly round the plants with a potting stick and leave 2 inches from the top of the pot to allow for top-dressing. It's always advisable to put the canes to the plants before you stand them outside, as they're so easily broken off with the wind. Sharpen the ends of the canes first and put them in the new soil, try to avoid pushing them in near the plant or you will damage the roots. They will want very careful watering for the first few weeks.

JULY

IN the cool of the evening there's no doubt that everything in the garden looks fresher and brighter than at any other time, and it is nice to weigh up the progress or otherwise of the crops or flowers, as well as to decide on which are the more important jobs to be tackled next.

Scented Flowers. Even more pleasing on a summer evening is the scent of the flowers. You know, scent is half the beauty of a garden. I always like to plant flowers noted for their beautiful scent near to a garden seat, by the side of a path or under a window. Roses, of course, are well known for their scent, but there are many of the more simple flowers with a really delightful scent, too. I wouldn't be without the flowering tobacco plant, nicotiana; the strongest scent undoubtedly comes from the white variety; and this has a tendency to close its flowers during the brightest part of the day and open them in the evening, but the variety Crimson Bedder is a lovely variety. There are, of course, other colours and hybrids which don't close their flowers during the day-time. Mignonette is not a striking flower and doesn't catch the eye like many others, but it has a lovely scent.

A plant we do not hear so much of or don't see grown so much these days is the night-scented stock, or, to give it its proper name, *Matthiola bicornis*. This, again, is not a flower which catches the eye, but in the evenings there's no mistaking the scent given off by these plants. It's a very easy plant to grow, and just a few seeds scattered in odd corners or under the shrubs and just raked into the surface is all that is necessary. It can be sown up to the middle of this month.

Plants for Shade. No garden should be without some form of shade or shelter. But, you know, it is often a problem to some people to know what to plant under the shade of a tree or in a part of the garden which is overshadowed by buildings. Some gardens, particularly in the towns where they are surrounded by buildings, hardly get a glimpse of the sun. If it is due to over-hanging trees, at this time of the year it is possible to assess the density of the shade or otherwise. Trees with large leaves throw a very heavy shade, while under those with smaller leaves and many of the ornamental flowering trees the shade is much less dense. When you visit your friends and neighbours' gardens it is well worth making a note of those shrubs and plants you see growing and enjoying the shade of trees or buildings. It is, of course, not always shade that is the deciding factor; many plants and shrubs which normally enjoy shade fail under trees because of the lack of moisture.

If you intend planting under large trees, then the soil must be dug first and some manure or compost worked into the soil to help retain the moisture and assist the plants to compete with the tree roots and get themselves established. To list a few shrubs: firstly, you will notice that most berberis will grow in the shade. The *Hypericum calycinum*, more commonly known as St John's Wort, with those attractive yellow poppy-like flowers, when once established will grow and flower quite freely through-out most of the summer. Rhododendrons and azaleas appreciate shade, but these must have a soil which suits them. It is a miser-able sight to see one of these trying to survive in a soil which it doesn't like. There must be no lime in the soil whatsoever.

Among the other shade-loving plants I would include Solo-mon's seal, lily of the valley, the hardy primulas where it is moist, foxgloves (there are now some wonderful varieties of these), and *Meconopsis Baileyi*, that beautiful Himalayan poppy. This is an attractive plant and is becoming very popular. If you have a friend who has a few of these growing and flowering in his garden, ask him for one of the seed pods. They seed very freely and seeds sown as soon as they're ripe will germinate like mustard and cress; if they're kept for any length of time they deteriorate very quickly. Some of the seedlings from seed sown early this month will flower next year, and I know you would be proud to have them in your garden. The seed of foxgloves can be sown this month, too. Some of the new hybrids in white, cream, pink and other colours are well worth having in the garden. **Prick out Seedlings.** Then, from the middle of the month on-ward the seedlings of those wallflowers, sweet Williams, forget-

me-nots and others from the seed we sowed last month will be
ready for pricking out. Whatever you do don't leave them in the
seed rows, they'll all be fighting for light and air and will get
drawn and weak. Prick them out while they're still small on a
piece of spare ground, 9 inches apart each way, and if the soil is
dry, water them in well to help them to get established.

Annuals. Geraniums, salvias and quite a lot of the annuals
often make a lot of leaf-growth at the expense of flower; this
usually happens in damp showery weather, with little sunshine.
In such seasons, a little potash will often correct the balance of
growth and improve the quantity and quality of the flowers. You
can dissolve a dessertspoonful, no more, of sulphate of potash in
a gallon of water, and water round the plants with this, but be
sure to keep it off the foliage and the stems.

Roses. Keep all the dead flowers picked off, and when you take
the dead roses off don't just pull off the flower-heads, get a pair of
sécateurs and do the job properly, because, you know, you want
more roses in August, September and October. Cut away about
a third to a half of the growth which has been produced this
year, make a clean cut immediately above a leaf-joint and you
will soon see the new young growths coming which will provide
your later flowers. A light sprinkling of a good fertilizer round
each bush, stirred in to the soil, will give them that bit of en-
couragement. If you see any sign of mildew on the rambler roses
or climbers spray them straight away with a colloidal sulphur
spray before it spoils too many of the flowers.

Propagating Shrubs. Of course, this month is the best time to
propagate any of your favourite flowering shrubs. You may be
thinking to yourself, 'Well, that's beyond me, I haven't elaborate propagating frames for this kind of thing'. It doesn't matter if
you haven't a frame at all. You'll possibly need only one or two
of each kind, and these you can propagate quite easily in an ordinary box. Get one that's about 8 or 9 inches deep; if there isn't
any space between the boards on the bottom make a few holes, so
that any surplus water can drain away, put the box out in the
garden and fill it half full with fairly coarse sand—and this you
will be able to get from your nearest sand quarry or from a
builders' merchant. I think it's what the builder calls concreting
sand; all you need then is a sheet or two of glass to put over the

top of the box to keep the atmosphere inside close and moist.

Now cuttings. If it's shrubs, they needn't be more than from 2 to 4 inches long. Choose the growths which have been made during this season, that is, the young growths. Pull them off the main stem and they will have at the bottom end what the gardener calls a 'heel'. With a sharp knife just trim off the loose ends of bark and wood as well as a few of the bottom leaves. You'll find they will root quicker if you get one of the hormone rooting powders, and all you have to do is to dip the bottom half-inch of the cuttings firstly in water and then into the rooting powder, and they're ready to go into the box. Put the cuttings about half their length into the sand and give the box a really good watering. Put the glass over the top and a light piece of material or newspaper over the glass to shade them from the sunlight. The sand, of course, does not retain much moisture, so it will be necessary to water them thoroughly every few days, because at no time must they be allowed to get dry. Most of the cuttings will be rooted in six to eight weeks, and then they must either be planted out in the garden and kept watered, or potted off singly into pots. As soon as they're rooted they must come out of the sand, because there is little or no plant food in it for them.

Hanging Baskets.   Don't forget that the hanging basket over the front door wants watering every day, rain or no rain, and a little weak liquid fertilizer at least once a week. If you're going away for your holiday I'm sure the neighbour would water it for you.

WORK IN THE GREENHOUSE AND FRAME

Cyclamen.   The cyclamen in the frame can be sprayed over with clear water morning and night; they love it, and it helps to keep them clean. They should be shaded during the day-time, and once they have got over that move into the final pots I like to take the frame lights off at night-time. Keep a watch for thrips and greenfly.

Chrysanthemums.   The chrysanthemums should be making good root in their final pots and will gradually take more and more water. If they had a good soil mixture I don't think it's wise to commence feeding until towards the end of the month, and then not more than once a fortnight at first. They appreciate a spray overhead morning and night, particularly in warm dry weather.

Final potting of a chrysanthemum. After the pot has been crocked and a layer of rough drainage material put in place, I put some compost in and place the plant in position as shown above. I put more compost in and ram this firmly with a stick, all round the pot, as shown in the photograph below.

Final potting of a chrysanthemum. *Above:* I use three stout stakes or canes, and then finally fill the pot with well-rammed compost, leaving a couple of inches or so at the top for top-dressing and for watering. *Below:* Finally, I loop raffia round the canes as shown.

Potting on young primula plants. *Above:* I carefully remove the plants from the box, using a hand fork, taking care not to damage the roots, and retaining as much soil as possible. *Below:* I then pot them into individual pots, adding a little compost at a time.

Above left: Potting primulas. I firm the compost with my fingers. *Above right:* I find that a light sprinkling of fertilizer round the roses will encourage further growth. I also remove dead flower heads (*below left*) cutting just above a bud, to encourage new growths. *Below right:* Removing a shoot with a heel, for propagation. Many shrubs can be propagated by cuttings of this type.

64

AUGUST

DON'T forget to make notes of any alterations for the herbaceous border. Now is the time to note any alterations you want to make while the border is in flower. Don't trust to memory, it can be very unreliable, and if you should forget you will have to put up with it for a further twelve months.

Early-flowering Chrysanthemums. In the flower garden the border chrysanthemums should be making headway. Keep them tied to their supports. It is important over the next few weeks that disbudding and feeding should be carefully attended to. Let's discuss disbudding first.

Securing the Buds. The plants will want looking over at least twice a week and the buds secured before the side-shoots get too far advanced; don't let them get an inch or two long before you remove them, otherwise the buds will not come away as freely as you will want them to. Remove all the side-buds and side-shoots for about 12 or 18 inches down the stem, sufficient to give you a good stem for cutting. Leave the side-shoots below this, as these will provide you with good flowers for cutting in late September and October, and at that time, even if you are keen on showing, they will be useful for indoor decoration and, of course, help you to keep your stripes, as you are bound to lose them when you take all the best blooms off to the show. Be careful not to damage the foliage in any way as, after all, the leaves are the lungs of the plant and good, clean, healthy foliage adds a lot to what may already be a first-class bloom.

Protect against Wind. Make sure the plants are protected against wind damage, and if you can put three or four stakes round each plant so much the better; with only one stake the wind blows the growths backwards and forwards and round the cane, and a lot of the growths are broken off or the blooms badly bruised.

Feeding. Now, the feeding of the plants. They should be ready for feeding once a week and a question that is always asked is, 'What shall I feed them with?' Well, there are many proprietary brands of chrysanthemum fertilizer on the market, but don't you be misled because a certain one is called somebody's 'extra-special'. Delve a little deeper into it and find out what the analysis is; you are entitled to ask for this, and compare it with other fertilizers, which may perhaps be cheaper and yet just as good, if not better.

The first thing to look for is the potash content, as this is important for fineness in the flower and richness in colour. You want a fertilizer which is guaranteed to contain nothing less than 6% of potash, with 5% or a little more of nitrogen and 3 to 5% of soluble phosphate. Ignore the amount of insoluble phosphate, as this is of little or no value to you for immediate use. Don't think you will beat the other fellow by giving the plants heavy dressings; you won't, you may find you will be further behind in the long run. A dessertspoonful sprinkled round each plant, well away from the stem, once a week is quite sufficient; either stir it into the topsoil or water it in and, if the weather is dry, give them all the water you can.

Watch for Pests.   Watch them for the capsid bug, as this little brute can do untold damage. He always goes for the young tips and young buds and the result of his mischief is often not seen until much later when the buds, perhaps, open only on one side and come badly deformed; spraying or dusting with DDT will keep him at bay, and also the earwigs.

Protecting Blooms.   Now, what about the blooms? Some varieties get scorched badly with the sun and some mark badly with the rain, particularly some of the whites. Those for the exhibition table will pay for protection, either by shaded frame lights over the plants, or by thin paper bags over the individual blooms, but don't keep them too much from the light or the colour will be poor, and that is often the deciding factor when competition is keen.

Late-flowering Chrysanthemums.   Now for the late-flowering chrysanthemums—those that you will be putting in the greenhouse from mid-September onward. Let's have a look at the large exhibition and incurved varieties first. During this month it will be necessary to secure the buds if they are to be in time for the November shows.

Disbudding. These, like the early-flowering border chrysanthemums, should be disbudded as soon as the side-buds are large enough to rub out. The incurved varieties will be a bit later in showing their buds. I have noticed on the Curry varieties that they throw a late natural break, but with these particular varieties, with a little care, you can't go wrong, they will be in time. I would say they're about the easiest of them all. If you secure your buds too early on these varieties I don't think you get that fineness in the bloom that is so essential for incurves, the blooms tend to be rather rough and coarse. The foliage on these and the large exhibition should now have that dark luscious look about it. I'm often asked why the Majestic varieties go yellow in the foliage after they have been potted in their final pots. They nearly always do, I know, it seems to be peculiar to that variety and to its sports; it usually happens when the plants are moved from the greenhouse to the frame, or from the frame to outside. It may be due to change of temperature, but I think more often than not to over-watering or a lot of rain, particularly after the plants have been put in their final pots, that's the time when the greatest care should be taken in watering, and always err on the dry side until the plants get established in the new soil. I find that the yellowing disappears once the plants are well rooted in their final pots.

The decorative and single varieties should now be making their flowering growth, but the buds shouldn't be too evident before the later part of the month or early September.

Feeding. By now they should all have made sufficient root to take their first feed, say every ten days to begin with, and gradually increase it to once a week; again I expect the question arises, 'Well, what shall I use?' All I can say is use a balanced fertilizer, such as I have recommended for the early-flowering chrysanthemums, one which contains potash, nitrogen and phosphate in fair proportions. The next thing is how to use it, and I must again say, use it carefully.

When you potted your chrysanthemums in their final pots you should have left ample room for top-dressing, so mix 1 part of the manure with 2 parts of fine soil and give each pot a small handful sprinkled evenly over the surface, and well water it in. I always find this the best way of feeding, and it's the way the experts tell us to feed.

Keep all the growths tied to their supports, and canes tied to a wire stranded between two strong posts, because, as the amount of top growth increases, there is more likelihood of the plants being blown over and broken.

Dahlias.   The dahlias will soon be at their best. Watch them for earwig damage. Keep them watered and tied in, and if you want them for showing some disbudding will be necessary, with the exception of the pompons. They are better not disbudded, as for this type you want a small neat flower, not more than 2 inches across; if you disbud they tend to come larger and be rather rough.

Sweet Peas.   The sweet peas should be cut as often as possible, never let them go to seed, and keep them well supplied with water and liquid manure.

Bulbs for Christmas Flowering.   If we want bulbs in flower for Christmas then that's another job we must give attention to this month, without fail. For this we don't need to wait for a good rain. Get your bulb catalogue out or visit your seedsman as soon as you can, because for Christmas flowering you do want specially prepared bulbs, and they must be given good time to make plenty of root before you begin to force them into flower

Possibly one of the best and easiest to get into flower in time for Christmas is the Roman Hyacinth, its small white flowers are very attractive and the scent is really delightful. It is possible to get the specially prepared hyacinths too, I see listed such varieties as Bismarck, a good light blue, Pink Pearl and Jan Bos, a bright red. Refrigerated daffodil bulbs should be put in pots or bowls immediately they are received, and must be ordered before the middle of August, and while the flowering time given for King Alfreds is January the fifteenth, Magnificent, a large yellow trumpet variety, is December the twenty-third. Golden Harvest is a good one and the flowering time given for that is December the twenty-ninth. Helios is another good daffodil and can be got in flower by January the second.

It is very difficult to get tulips in flower for Christmas, but a few pots or bowls are well worth while, particularly the double-flowering ones for flowering in January and February. We should always plan for succession, and then, of course, we mustn't forget the crocus, scillas and the snowdrop.

Planting the Bulbs. If we're growing our bulbs in bowls with no drainage, then we must use the specially prepared fibre compost which can be bought at any garden sundriesman or seed store. The fibre should be well moistened before it is used and should never be allowed to get dry during the growing period, nor must it be made sodden or the bulbs will decay instead of growing. We must give only sufficient water to keep the fibre moist. I always like to put a few lumps of charcoal in the bottom of the bowl first and cover them with about 2 inches of the fibre. Next we place our bulbs in position, leaving an inch or two between each bulb. The number of bulbs to put in the bowl will, of course, depend on the size of the bowl and the size of the bulbs. A bowl large enough to take three hyacinths would be large enough for six tulips or the smaller narcissi, or twelve of such bulbs as the crocus or snowdrop. The bowl can then be filled with the fibre almost to the rim, and it will not matter if the nose or top of the larger bulbs is showing; in fact, for hyacinths in particular, I prefer to have the top of the bulb above the fibre. The fibre can be made firm but not tight round the bulbs.

For growing in flower-pots I like to use the standard potting compost, because in this case we're providing good drainage by putting a few pieces of broken pot in the bottom and there's not the likelihood of getting this too wet once the bulbs have made good root.

Encouraging Root Growth. That brings me back to the importance of encouraging root growth before we bring the pots or bowls into the greenhouse or into a warm room to force them into growth; in any case, they won't force well and produce good flowers unless they have made good root. They should be placed in a cool dark place for about eight weeks, and if you can bury them in clean ashes or sand so that there's two or three inches above the pots, so much the better. During this time they will make their root, they can then be brought out into the light and air, and from then on light is most essential: I would go so far as to say that lack of light is the cause of more failures than anything else.

WORK IN THE GREENHOUSE AND FRAME

Sow Schizanthus.   This month is the time to sow your schizanthus for flowering next April and May. Sow the seed in pots or boxes and lightly cover it with fine soil. Put them in a cold frame and shade them until you see the young seedlings appear, then give them all the light and air you can. As soon as they are large enough to handle, pot them off into small pots. Never subject them to artificial heat, they don't like it; all they will require all through the winter is just sufficient to keep out the frost.

SEPTEMBER

ONE thing that impresses me at the shows is the popularity of the floral decoration classes. This popularity has undoubtedly been on the increase over the past five or six years. When we see as many as forty or fifty entries in a class, surely it speaks for itself. It is certainly very nice to see this, because this is more or less the ladies' section, and we are bound to see the benefit of this reflected in the home with better-arranged flowers.

Flowers for Cutting. There is an art in using a mere six or dozen flowers and making an attractive arrangement with the addition of some suitable foliage, instead of just pushing them into a vase. It means, too, that there is an increasing demand for cut flowers. Now, like most gardeners I am not in favour of cutting from the beds and borders round the house, they have been planted to beautify the surroundings. Instead, a part of the garden should be set aside especially for the growing of flowers for cutting.

In that part of the garden there could be a few bulbs and other spring flowers. These could be followed by some of the annuals, those which are suitable for this purpose. Then there are the herbaceous perennials, such as scabious, alstroemeria (the Peruvian Lily), helenium, montbretia and others, gladioli and chrysanthemums, and a few roses to save cutting those near the house.

In the sheltered parts of the country many of the hardy annuals can be sown outside in the autumn. They will come safely through the winter and begin to flower during the late spring and early summer. In fact, this month is the ideal time to sow them. The best ones for cutting include cornflower, larkspur, annual scabious, calendula, godetia, clarkia and possibly the most popular of all, the sweet pea. The seed can be sown thinly in drills on a sheltered border, and if you think the position is rather exposed you can, before the winter sets in, push in to the soil along each side of the rows a few thin twiggy pieces of stick: these make a fine windbreak.

Ixias are not known and grown as much as they might be, you know. They are beautiful for cutting and you can get them in either named varieties or mixed colours. They are quite hardy and the bulbs can be planted this month for flowering in May, June and July of next year. You will, I am sure, have seen their very attractive spikes of flower with thin rather wiry stems in white, pink and purple on sale in the shops and markets. Daffodil and narcissi bulbs are all the better if planted this month too.

Foliage. A moment ago I mentioned foliage for the flower arrangement. It is very essential to have good foliage, and particularly the coloured and variegated foliage. The funkia or plantain lily has a large and very useful leaf. The ordinary garden variety has a greyish or bluish sheen and there are some with variegated foliage. There is the silver-foliage lavender cotton or, to give it its proper name, santolina. The *Senecio Greyi* has silvery foliage. Some of the ivies have variegated foliage, and the euonymus, too. Bronze or copper foliage is often used, and there is the purple-leaved plum, *Prunus Pissardii*, with bronze foliage, hazel and rhus and, of course, the Japanese maples. You do not need me to remind you of those shrubs which have good autumn tints and berries. The time for planting these is during October and November.

If you have a greenhouse then the rather exotic foliage of the *Begonia Rex* and other plants is very useful. The time has come, I am sure, when every garden should provide flowers and foliage for use in the house without having to rob the ornamental part.

Cuttings. I have already mentioned that certain plants will not reproduce true to type from seed, and this applies not only when it is saved at home but when it is saved and collected by the specialists too, and I am referring especially to flowering plants. It is for this reason that the gardener has to keep his stock from year to year by taking cuttings, and he is sure then that each plant will be exactly the same in type, colour and habit as the parent plant. It is what we call vegetative propagation: plants propagated in this way include the geraniums, fuchsias, penstemons, calceolarias and some of the violas.

Let us take the geraniums first, because these must be rooted before the end of October if they are to come safely through the

think begonias are splendid for hanging baskets. Don't forget to keep the baskets well watered, particularly in hot weather. Never let them get dry.

Above: Securing the chrysanthemum bud. I never let the side-shoots get too lo~
before removing them otherwise the crown bud will not develop freely. I remo~
side-buds and side-shoots for about 18 inches down the stem. *Below:* I like ~
protect choice blooms against sun scorch and rain, with thin paper bags.

Christmas bulbs. Prepared Roman hyacinths can be flowered at Christmas time if you plant the bulbs in August. Plant them in bowls, pots, or pans, in bulb fibre, with their noses just showing (*above*). Place them in a north-facing position outside and cover them with clean ashes or sand.

Above: Cutting gladioli. I insert a knife low down into the stem and move th
spike gently first one way and then the other holding the base firm with the oth
hand. The spike will snap and can easily be withdrawn. *Below:* Preparing an
inserting geranium cuttings. Trim the cuttings below a joint and insert them i
sandy compost to root.

Lifting dahlias. When frost blackens the stems in the autumn dahlias should be lifted for storing. I cut off the dead haulm 6 inches or so above soil level, lift the tubers, with a fork, shake off surplus soil, label them and store them in a dry, frost-proof place until they are required for cuttings or for planting out next year.

Above: Planting out forget-me-nots. I plant mine out in October for sprin
display, but before planting I rake in a light dressing of bonemeal and firm th
soil. *Below:* Planting a tree. Make a large enough hole, and spread out the root
The stick acts as a guide to the correct planting depth.

Above: I find that a pot tapper is useful for testing pots to see whether they require watering. *Below:* Pruning rambler roses. I cut away much of the old growth on the left, leaving, on the right, the new growths and some of the older growths, to flower next year.

Above: Putting the tender plants to bed. I use a layer of bracken held in place with canes to protect crowns of eremurus and other tender plants. This must be removed carefully to avoid damage to young growths, when the danger of frost is over. *Below:* On frosty nights mats spread over the frame lights will prevent frost damage.

winter. Well-matured shoots make the best cuttings and those that are mature enough to produce flowers will root quite easily and make good plants. They need not be more than 4 or 5 inches long. Remove the one or two bottom leaves and cut straight across immediately below a leaf-joint. They can be put straight into the garden frame or into pots and boxes filled with sandy soil and stood under a sheltered wall in the garden, but they will have to be brought inside before the frosts begin.

The best shoots to choose on the calceolarias and penstemons are those which have not produced a flower, and on the violas those young shoots from the base of the plants, not those hollow flowering growths—these never make good plants. All these can go into the garden frame or a box, and with a little protection will be quite safe for the winter. They are almost hardy.

Housing Chrysanthemums.   Towards the end of the month the earliest ones will have to be brought inside. I like to see them inside just before they begin to unfold their petals.

WORK IN THE GREENHOUSE AND FRAME

Annuals for Spring Display.   Have you ever thought of growing hardy annuals as pot plants for flowering in the spring and early summer? I can assure you that many of them do exceptionally well and make a very fine display in the greenhouse and I, for one, wouldn't be without them. With just the ordinary care that we make a habit of giving to all our plants we grow in pots, they're quite easy and they don't require high temperatures during the winter months; it does them more harm than good.

Let's first of all consider those which are most suited for growing in this way. I would choose the Beauty of Nice stock, larkspur, nemesia, clarkia, salpiglossis and the antirrhinum which, although we nearly always grow it as an annual, is strictly speaking a perennial. They will all make fine pot plants and give you a really colourful display in the greenhouse in spring.

For the average greenhouse you will need only a small packet of seed of each, or of those which are your particular favourites, and as this is the month for sowing them perhaps it would be as well if we discuss their requirements for a few moments. Sow the seed thinly in pots or boxes, just the same as you did in the spring, when you used a good layer of broken pot in the bottom of the boxes for drainage, a soil mixture of 2 parts of loam which had been passed through the $\frac{1}{2}$-inch riddle, 1 part of peat and 1 part of sand, with $1\frac{1}{2}$ oz. of superphosphate and $\frac{3}{4}$ oz. of lime to each bushel of the mixture. If you remember, this was made firm and level in the boxes or pots and well watered before sowing. The seed was then sprinkled thinly over the surface and just covered with a sprinkling of fine soil. As each box is sown it should be labelled and then placed in the garden frame with a sheet of paper put over it until the seeds begin to show through the soil, which will perhaps be a week to ten days. You will no doubt find that they will not want watering again until the seedlings are well through the soil; even then they should be watered only as the soil gets dry. They should be given all the light and air possible, because we've got to remember they're all sun-loving plants and with plenty of air round them they will make those nice sturdy plants which will come through the winter unharmed.

As soon as the seedlings are large enough to handle they can be transferred to their first pots, which shouldn't be larger than a $3\frac{1}{2}$-inch: use the same soil mixture and put a few crocks in the bottom of the pots for drainage, as this is more important at this time of the year than at any time. I will tell you what I do. I fill the pots to the top and then just lightly firm the soil with the fingers so that the surface of the soil is about half an inch below the top, then I get a small wooden dibber and prick the plants out three in each pot, evenly spaced out. I give them a good watering and put the pots on a shelf in the greenhouse as near to the glass as possible. They want very careful watering all through the winter, because if you give them too much you'll kill them; in fact, I like to keep them rather on the dry side.

They can remain in these pots until January, and then pot them on in to 5- or 6-inch pots, in which they will flower. For this potting use a slightly richer mixture, the John Innes potting mixture which has 4 oz. of base manure instead of the superphosphate. They will still want careful watering and plenty of light and air. As soon as the pots are full of root you can give them a little fertilizer, about 1 oz. to the gallon of water every fortnight.

OCTOBER

IN the flower garden it is time we began changing over from summer to spring bedding; the wallflowers, polyanthus, forget-me-nots, aubrietas, winter-flowering pansies, sweet Williams and others should be in their flowering quarters before the month is out. This will give them a chance to settle down before winter really sets in.

Planting Spring Bedding Plants. Now there are a few observations I would like to make with regard to the planting. The first is that as soon as the beds or borders are cleared the soil should be well turned over with a garden spade. Next, it is just as important to firm the soil now as it was when we were planting in the spring. You could give it a light sprinkling of bonemeal before you rake it down, the bonemeal would be available to the plants when they begin their growth in the spring. Another very important thing is not to lift the plants before you are ready for planting, they should be lifted carefully with as much soil on the roots as possible and planted straight away. If they are left hanging about with their roots exposed to the air they take a long time to recover.

The distance of planting will vary according to the plant, forget-me-nots, polyanthus and winter-flowering pansies can be planted about 9 inches apart; wallflowers, sweet Williams and aubrietas can be 12 to 15 inches apart. They will easily fill this amount of space when they begin to throw their flowers in the spring. Do give them a good planting—do not forget they have the winter months ahead of them; make each hole large enough; plant them, if anything, a little deeper than they were when you lifted them and press the soil very firmly round each one. Make a really first-class job of it because, you know, you will be looking at your job each time you go into the garden, and there will not be other flowers to take your attention from those plants you have put in. When you are planting you will want to straighten your back occasionally; well, that is the time to just step back and see if you are making a nice neat job of it.

Lifting Dahlias.   Now the dahlias. The first nip of frost and their tops will be blackened, and even if we do not get a nip it would be wise to lift the tubers before the end of the month. Look over them and make sure each one is labelled before the last flowers go. It is so important when you are planting them out in the spring to know the height, colour, type, etc. Any that have shown signs of being stunted or diseased should be discarded and the remainder lifted carefully with as little damage to the tubers as possible. Clean off the bulk of the soil, dry the tubers and store them in straw or under sacking in a frost-proof room or shed. The same conditions under which potatoes are stored is ideal. It is, of course, very important that the tubers should not be frosted, otherwise they will not start away in the spring.

Saving Half-hardy Plants.   Any of the other half-hardy summer-flowering plants which we want to save should also be lifted and brought in before we get a frost. Among these are geraniums, fuchsias, heliotrope, begonias and some of the foliage plants, such as abutilon, centaurea and the silver leucophytum. Some of our bedding plants, you know, such as the fibrous-rooted begonias, if lifted carefully, potted and put in the greenhouse will continue to flower late into the winter and will give us a nice bit of colour when flowers are becoming scarce and expensive: it is nice to be able to have a few flowering plants for the house in the dark days of winter.

Lifting Gladioli.   The gladioli will want lifting and drying, and the corms cleaned and stored away from the frost. There is a disease which is becoming very prevalent among the gladioli: it can be distinguished by the very early yellowing of the foliage, the plant often failing to flower and dying down early; these should be lifted and burnt immediately these symptoms are seen, as it spreads very rapidly.

Take Cuttings.   Cuttings of the bedding calceolaria, penstemon, viola, etc., can still be taken. All they need during the winter is the protection of a cold frame with a straw or mat covering during the very severest weather. Keep the frame closed for a few weeks until the cuttings have rooted.

Planting Trees and Shrubs.   Evergreen trees and shrubs establish themselves better if the planting of these is left until March or April, but all the deciduous trees and shrubs, roses, climbers and fruit trees are all the better for autumn planting. We always consider October and November to be the best months; you see, at this time of the year the soil is still warm and they have a chance to settle in their new surroundings and begin to make root before the worst of the winter weather sets in, and as soon as we get the spring sunshine they are ready to start into new growth.

I am quite certain that far too often there is not enough time and care given to planting things in the garden, and there are far more losses than there need be, due to faulty planting. You know, it is not a matter of just making a hole and putting the roots in. If we buy half a dozen rose trees or a few shrubs we want to see them grow and enjoy the pleasure of looking at them for years to come. We must be prepared to give them a good chance and a fair start, or we cannot expect them to grow and flower, can we? As we are getting near to planting-time I think it will be well worth our while to discuss some of the main principles of planting.

When we dig a plant from the garden or, for that matter, if the nurseryman from whom we are buying our plants does, it is impossible to do it without disturbing the roots, and it is bound to be a shock to the plant. Now it is up to us to see that we reduce that shock to a minimum, and there are a number of ways in which we can. Whether it be a herbaceous plant or a shrub, it must be lifted from the soil with as little damage or disturbance to the roots as possible; the spade or fork—and preferably the fork—must be put in as far away from the stem as possible. Work well round the plant before you begin to lift, and any roots you can find, follow them as far as you can, that is why I say I prefer a fork to a spade, it is so easy to cut through the roots with a spade. If you are moving a plant from one part of the garden to another then have the hole partially prepared before you lift, the roots do not want to be out of the soil any longer than is absolutely necessary. Do not expose them to drying winds, they like to be kept moist; in fact, at no time should they be allowed to get dry, and any plants, trees or shrubs which have to travel any distance should be well packed to prevent the roots from drying. If you have ordered yours from away and the roots are dry on arrival, stand them in water for up to twelve hours before you plant, they will be all the better for it.

Now what about the planting? I am always telling people never to plant unless the condition of the soil is right. What do we mean by right conditions. Well, on no account must the soil be wet and sticky. I do not like to see it sticking to the boots, but that might be a bit too fussy. Certainly it would not be in a good condition if frost were in the ground. The soil should crumble down easily and yet be moist. If the soil is dry, then it is an easy matter to water after planting, but never before. If your plants arrive when the soil is wet and sticky, or if it is not possible for you to plant them straight away, there is no need for them to be left out of the soil in the meantime, heel them in somewhere in the garden so that all the roots are covered until you can plant them.

The depth of planting is, of course, important too. If we plant too deeply the roots are likely to be in cold wet soil and they will not like it; air is essential to the roots and if they are down too deep they will not get the air they need. If they are planted too shallowly they will get dry in windy and sunny weather and the plants will take a long time to get established. It is very difficult to lay down any hard-and-fast rules; you see, some plants are naturally deeper rooting than others, and soil conditions will often make all the difference; for instance, plants growing in a light soil will often go deeper in search of moisture, while in heavier soils the same plants may be much shallower rooting. If you buy fruit trees, roses or shrubs, it is always a good guide to plant the same depth as they were planted previously, it is quite easy to tell this if you look at the stems. I would go so far as to say that for the average young tree or shrub no roots need to be deeper than about 9 inches, and the young fibrous roots spread out so that they are not more than 3 or 4 inches below the surface. I hope I have made that clear.

The size of the hole, of course, will depend on the root spread of your plant. It should be large enough to enable you to spread all the roots in an outward direction without cramping. If it is a fruit tree, or anything else which will need a support, put the stake in before you plant, otherwise, if you drive it in after planting, the roots may be damaged.

Shake the soil through the roots as you fill in the hole and press the soil firmly; when you have completely filled in tread all round with the feet, because firm planting is one of the secrets of success. Unless you are planting against a wall where the soil is often dry it is not necessary to water at this time of the year. but one question I'm often asked is, 'Is it advisable to put manure in the hole?' On no account should manure, whatever it is, be in direct contact with the roots. It can be mixed with the soil at the bottom of the hole, or with that for filling it, the roots will find it when they are ready.

WORK IN THE GREENHOUSE

The cyclamen, primula and cineraria which have been in the cold frame could now be moved to the more congenial atmosphere of the greenhouse and will want watering with great care. It is a good idea to have a cotton-reel on the end of a cane and tap the pots. You will soon become accustomed to picking out the dry ones by a distinctive ring compared with a more dull sound from the pots which do not require watering. If the pots are full of root give them a little weak liquid manure occasionally. The house should not be closed down and the plant should not be subjected to high temperatures. Give them all the ventilation you can for a few weeks and damp the floors of the greenhouse on bright days.

NOVEMBER

LOOKING round the garden at this time of the year I cannot help but admire the autumn tints, particularly on the shrubs, and where there are berries to add to the colour it is a really delightful picture. It makes me realize more than ever that when planting shrubs we must not be content with just flowers in spring and summer, but look a little further ahead and choose shrubs which will give us these delightful colours in autumn as well.

Some Good Plants for Colouring. I am particularly impressed with *Berberis Wilsonae*, with its long drooping branches covered in masses of coral-red berries and the lovely tints of the foliage. How nice that shrub looks when in flower during late June and early July.

Another very bright one is *Rhus Cotinus*, often known as the smoke plant. The foliage of this is a bright orange-scarlet, and this particular shrub creates a lot of interest during the summer when it is covered in a pinkish feathery mass, afterwards turning grey and looking all the world like a puff of smoke.

On the rock garden *Cotoneaster horizontalis* is as bright as any. Here is a shrub that is quite at home on the rock garden, in the front of a shrub border, and is an ideal wall shrub, I cannot leave the shrubs on the rock garden without a mention of the Japanese maples. They never fail to give good autumn colour, and *Acer palmatum dissectum* is exceptionally good.

Flowers are often already showing on *Viburnum fragrans*. It is a particular favourite of mine. It will continue to show its pinky-white flowers all through the winter and when brought into a warm room the scent is delightful.

As a wall shrub the fire thorn, *Pyracantha Lalandii*, is one worth remembering. It is covered in one mass of orange-scarlet berries and these will remain bright like this until the birds take a fancy to them, which they usually do in early December.

Pruning Rambler Roses. The plant that I find more neglected than any other, so far as pruning is concerned, is the rambler rose. Now let me make it quite clear that I am not referring to the climbing roses, I mean those such as Dorothy Perkins, Albertine, Excelsa and the New Dawn. Any of this type which have not as yet been pruned can be done as soon as possible. Actually the best time to prune these, you know, is as soon as flowering has finished.

To do the pruning correctly just pause for a moment and think how they flower, and from which growths we get the finest flowers. I am sure you must have noticed how, during the summer, this particular type of rose sends up strong young growths from the base and, no doubt, you have been tempted to cut them off when the wife has complained about damage to the washing or possibly the nylons, or if they have caught your arm as you are working among your plants. I hope you did not cut them off, because it is these growths which provide that profusion of flowers the following year. They should be carefully tied back during the summer and trained on to the wall or trellis during the autumn or early winter.

When pruning your rambler rose remember the object should be to encourage as much young growth from the base as possible. A lot of the older growths, those that have flowered during the past summer, can be cut right out to ground-level, and to do this all the growths should firstly be brought down from the trellis or wall; select those that you will require for training back again, and these may have to include some of the older growths as well, and cut out the remainder. On the older growths you may have to leave will be side-growths, these can be pruned back to within about an inch of the main stem. Should there be, and there often are, long pieces of young growth coming from the older stems, these can be left if they are required to cover the allotted space.

When the pruning is finished all the growths remaining are then tied in to where they are required, and do not forget each long growth should be 12 to 15 inches apart. They will quite easily fill this space in the spring and summer with their new growths and flowers. You could sprinkle a little bonemeal or some other slow-acting manure on the soil round the rambler roses and this would help them with next year's flowering. There is no doubt the rambler rose is a most valuable climber, and it is well worth looking after and doing well.

Bulbs in Bowls.   Be sure to look at your bulbs which you put away in a cool dark place; those that have been there six or eight weeks will soon be ready for coming out to the light. Put them in a cool light place for a week or two, and then bring them in to somewhere where it is a little warmer. By gradually bringing them in to a warmer place you will find they will flower and last so much longer.

The Herbaceous Border.   Apart from a few of the later Michael-mas daisies all that remains on the herbaceous border is the stems and browning leaves of the plants which have given us so much pleasure during the summer and autumn months, and the garden will look much better if these are cut down to within an inch or so of the ground and the border generally cleaned up. Any alterations you have in mind here would be best left until February and March, but I do think it is worth while just lightly forking between the plants to give the border that nice fresh look. If you have on the border *Agapanthus umbellatus, Crinum Powellii* or any others which you know are inclined to be a bit tender, it is worth putting a little loose straw or bracken round them for protection during the winter. If you have kniphofia, the red-hot poker, on the border, tie the leaves together in a neat bundle, it will help to keep the water from lodging in the crowns, because this can be the cause of losing the plants.

WORK IN THE GREENHOUSE

The greenhouse is a comfortable place when the weather outside is not fit for working, you can always find a job. In the average small greenhouse at this time of the year I would say there would be the chrysanthemums, primulas and cyclamen, geranium cuttings as well as the old plants of the geraniums, schizanthus, possibly calceolarias and other annuals for flowering early next year, fuchsias and various odd plants of our particular favourites, so let us deal with them in their turn, shall we?

Chrysanthemums.   Firstly the chrysanthemums, and the earliest of these will be in full flower. Once they reach this stage there is nothing gained by further feeding—in fact, it will have a tendency to sour the soil, and this would be fatal to cuttings you will want from these plants later on. The later-flowering ones, such as the Favourites and others which are at the moment swelling their buds, will benefit by feeding at least once a week until they begin to open their flowers.

Cyclamen and Primulas. If the cyclamen and primulas are well rooted, a feed with a little liquid fertilizer once a week will help to keep them flowering until well into next year; you know, they are the most valuable winter-flowering plants we have. It is important with the cyclamen to keep any dead leaves pulled out, and I mean pulled out, because if you break the leaves or flowers off, the remaining parts of the stem will set up damp in the crown of the plant, and this can be harmful to future flowers. Each leaf or dead flower must be pulled right out from the base.

Geranium Cuttings. The geranium cuttings must be looked over occasionally and all dead leaves removed, or these will cause the cuttings to damp.

Annuals. The schizanthus and other annuals must be kept as near to the glass as possible, to keep them sturdy, and do not forget they do not appreciate a lot of artificial heat.

Fuchsias. Fuchsias can be allowed to dry off a little, they appreciate a period of rest, so allow the soil in the pots to dry; in fact, I would give them only very occasional waterings between now and January.

Finally, do be careful with the watering-can. Water only when the plants need it and, if possible, in the morning and not in the late afternoon.

DECEMBER

WHAT can we expect from the outside garden? I am continually stressing the value of the winter-flowering shrubs and plants in our gardens. The outside garden is not so dormant in December as we might think, and can be planted so as to produce a few flowers for the house.

Winter-flowering Plants. I suppose the best-known Christmas-flowering plant for outside is the Christmas rose, *Helleborus niger*. If this has been planted under a south wall and you can put a frame light or other form of protection over it early in the month, you will have some fine blooms by the twenty-fifth. *Iris stylosa* is yet another useful winter-flowering plant which likes being planted under a south or west wall. It will throw up its whitish-looking buds from December to March, and if these buds are pulled and put in water in a moderate room temperature they will open up a most beautiful pale blue in twelve to twenty-four hours.

An old favourite is the yellow winter-flowering *Jasminum nudiflorum*, some of the long green growths with the fat buds, cut about the middle of the month, will be in full flower for Christmas. That little gem *Erica darleyensis*, the winter-flowering heather, can always be relied on to show its deep rosy-pink flowers from November onwards.

Berberis Bealei, sometimes known as *Mahonia Bealei*, produces long racemes of lemon-yellow flowers with a lily-of-the-valley-like scent, and lasts well when cut and put into water; another good one we do not hear a great deal about is the winter-flowering cherry, *Prunus subhirtella autumnalis*. This tree shows its pinky-white flowers intermittently from late autumn onwards, and sprays cut and put into water in an ordinary room temperature will soon be covered in flowers and make a nice addition to many of your arrangements.

WORK IN THE GREENHOUSE AND FRAME

Chrysanthemum Cuttings.   In the greenhouse it will be time this month to put the first of the chrysanthemum cuttings in. I refer, of course, to the large-flowered exhibition varieties, often called Japanese chrysanthemums. If you grow them for exhibition some of the varieties will want 'stopping' in February and March, so you see it is essential to root them early. I have described the method of taking cuttings on page 10.

As the single and decorative chrysanthemums finish flowering cut them down to within about 18 inches from the base and keep them as near to the glass as possible. This is necessary if you are going to get good sturdy cuttings, you will find they will root easier and make much finer plants if you give them that little extra attention.

Controlling Humidity.   It is much more easy to control the humidity of the atmosphere in the greenhouse than it is in the frame, and it does want controlling during cold weather. A little warmth, however small the amount, will make all the difference, and there are today many improved greenhouse heaters at reasonable prices. One of those I have seen is an electric heater with an element similar to that in an electric kettle to heat water, and this was thermostatically controlled. A slightly more expensive one now on the market has a fan which circulates the warm air, and is also thermostatically controlled. The other way of controlling the humidity is, of course, by being very careful when using water; you do not want water on the floors and stagings when the temperature is very low, and always be very careful not to water any plant unless it is really dry—it does not matter if it gets to the point of flagging, it will be all the better for it.

Frames.   It can be a rather difficult time for plants in the garden frame, they may have to be covered at night with either straw or sacking to give them that extra protection, and on some days it is not wise to uncover them at all. This covering always causes a heavy, damp atmosphere in the frames. In fact you can often see the moisture hanging on the glass and round the sides of the frames. This is not good for plants, whether it be the roots of the outdoor-flowering chrysanthemums, geraniums which you are hoping to keep through the winter, calceolarias, penstemons or whatever it may be.

Whenever the weather is fine and not frosty it is always a good plan to either take the frame lights off for an hour or so each day, or prop the lights up a little to let in as much fresh air as possible. The plants will also want looking over because with being shut up for so long the conditions in the frame have been ideal for fungus or what the gardener calls damp. You will notice that any dead leaves will be covered in a mould, this will quickly affect other leaves, and any leaves or parts of plants affected in this way should be picked off and removed from the frame because this fungus, like many others, spreads by spores which float about in the atmosphere. This also applies to greenhouses, too, which are not heated, and sometimes in those which have got heat.

At this time of year it is always a sound policy to pick off any dead leaves there may be, particularly from the geraniums, or it will soon affect the stems, they will go black and you will lose the plants.

INDEX

95